The UNIVERSE, BLACK HOLES, and the BIG BANG

CRABTREE
Publishing Company
www.crabtreebooks.com

Crabtree Publishing Company
www.crabtreebooks.com
1-800-387-7650

Published in Canada
Crabtree Publishing
616 Welland Avenue
St. Catharines, ON
L2M 5V6

Published in the United States
Crabtree Publishing
PMB 59051
350 Fifth Ave, 59th Floor
New York, NY 10118

Author: Clive Gifford
Editorial director: Kathy Middleton
Editors: Izzi Howell, Shirley Duke
Designer: Clare Nicholas
Cover design and concept: Lisa Peacock
Proofreaders: Kathy Middleton
Prepress technician: Ken Wright
Print and production coordinator: Margaret Amy Salter

Published by Crabtree Publishing Company in 2016

First published in 2015 by Wayland
Copyright © Wayland, 2015

The website addresses (URLs) included in this book were valid at the time of going to press. However, it is possible that contents or addresses may have changed since the publication of this book. No responsibility for any such changes can be accepted by either the author or the Publisher.

Printed in the USA/082015/SN20150529

Picture credits:
Shutterstock/Vladimir Arndt cover (background), NASA/JPL-Caltech/Univ.of Ariz. cover (tl), Shutterstock/Antony McAulay cover (cr), Shutterstock/Lonely cover (bl), Shutterstock/jupeart cover (br), Shutterstock/Petrafler cover (br), Shutterstock/A-R-T title page (background), Shutterstock/Kotse title page (b).
NASA / WMAP Science Team 4, Shutterstock/RATOCA 5 (cr), Shutterstock/RedKoala 5 (bl), Thinkstock/Kanomdesign 5 (br), Science Photo Library/Mikkel Juul Jensen 6 (tl), Thinkstock/joaquin croxatto 6 (bl), Shutterstock/bioraven 7 (bl), Illustris Collaboration/Illustris Simulation 7 (br), Wikimedia 8 (tr), NASA / WMAP Science Team 8 (bl), Shutterstock/abstractdesignlabs 9 (tr), Shutterstock/bioraven 9 (cr), Dreamstime/ Thomas Jurkowski 9 (b), Science Photo Library/Mark Garlick 10-11, Stefan Chabluk 12 (including designs from Shutterstock/Macrovector and Shutterstock/veronchick84), Shutterstock/MW47 13 (bl), Shutterstock/Brent Hofacker 13 (br), ESA/NASA/Hubble 14 (tl), Wikimedia/Andrew Z. Colvin 14 (tc), NASA/JPL 14 (tr), A. Nota (ESA/STScI) et al., ESA, NASA 14 (bl), NASA/JPL-Caltech 14 (br), NASA, ESA, and the Hubble SM4 ERO Team 15 (tc), Shutterstock/RedKoala 15 (br), Science Photo Library/Mark Garlick 16, Shutterstock/RedKoala 17 (tr), NASA/JPL-Caltech 17 (tr), NASA/JPL-Caltech 18 (tl), NASA/CXC/M.Weiss 18 (br), Shutterstock/radmilla75 19 (cl), X-ray NASA/CXC/MIT/C.Canizares, M.Nowak; Optical NASA/STScI 19 (cr), X-ray: NASA/CXC/SAO; Optical: Rolf Olsen; Infrared: NASA/JPL-Caltech 20, Shutterstock/Skocko 21 (tr), Shutterstock/MichaelTaylor 21 (c), Shutterstock/sakkmesterke 22, Science Photo Library 23, NASA 24 (tl), NASA/JPL-Caltech 24 (bl), Shutterstock/RedKoala 24 (br), Shutterstock/Virinaflora 25 (cl), NASA, ESA, W. Keel (Univ. Alabama), et al., Galaxy Zoo Team 25 (cl), NASA 26 (tl), Shutterstock/bioraven 26 (br), NASA Ames/SETI Institute/JPL-Caltech 27 (tr), Shutterstock/RATOCA 27 (bl), NASA / WMAP Science Team 28, Shutterstock/Designua 29 (tr), Shutterstock/antishock 29 (bl), Shutterstock/bioraven 29 (br).

Design elements throughout: Shutterstock/Aphelleon, Shutterstock/PinkPueblo, Shutterstock/topform, Shutterstock/Nikiteev_Konstantin, Shutterstock/Elinalee, Shutterstock/mhatzapa, Shutterstock/notkoo, Shutterstock/Hilch. Shutterstock/CPdesign, Shutterstock/antoninaart.

Library and Archives Canada Cataloguing in Publication

Gifford, Clive, author
        The universe, black holes, and the big bang / Clive Gifford.

(Watch this space!)
Includes index.
Issued in print and electronic formats.
ISBN 978-0-7787-2024-9 (bound).--ISBN 978-0-7787-2028-7 (pbk.).--
ISBN 978-1-4271-1691-8 (pdf).--ISBN 978-1-4271-1687-1 (html)

        1. Cosmology--Juvenile literature. 2. Big bang theory--Juvenile
literature. 3. Black holes (Astronomy)--Juvenile literature.
        I. Title.

QB983.G54 2015   j523.1   C2015-903183-4
                                        C2015-903184-2

Library of Congress Cataloging-in-Publication Data

Gifford, Clive, author.
  The universe, black holes, and the Big Bang / Clive Gifford.
    pages cm. -- (Watch this space!)
  "First published in 2015 by Wayland."
  Includes index.
  ISBN 978-0-7787-2024-9 (reinforced library binding : alk. paper) --
ISBN 978-0-7787-2028-7 (pbk. : alk. paper) --
ISBN 978-1-4271-1691-8 (electronic pdf : alk. paper) --
ISBN 978-1-4271-1687-1 (electronic html : alk. paper)
  1. Cosmology--Juvenile literature. 2. Expanding universe--Juvenile literature.
3. Black holes (Astronomy)--Juvenile literature. 4. Universe--Juvenile
literature. I. Title.

QB983.G54 2016
523.1--dc23
                                        2015015367

CONTENTS

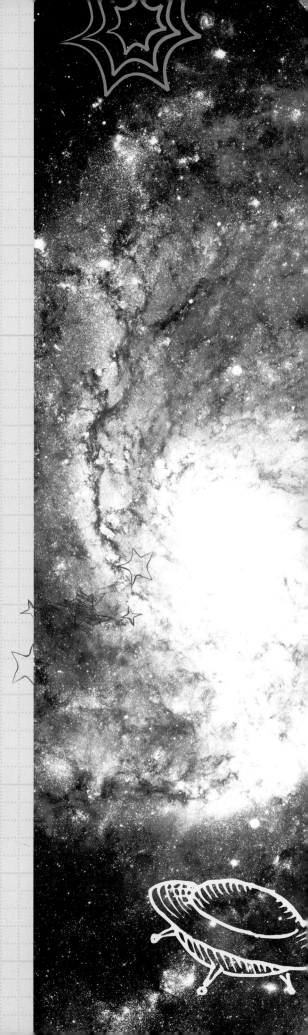

WHAT IS THE UNIVERSE?

The universe consists of absolutely everything we can see or sense, from the tiny particles inside an atom **to giant** galaxies **that take light millions of years to cross.**

Ancient Age

Cosmologists estimate that the universe is approximately 13.7 billion years old. This is a mind-blowingly long period of time. Humans are latecomers to the party, with our species, *Homo sapiens*, evolving on Earth just 200,000 years ago.

The Wilkinson Microwave Anisotropy Probe (WMAP) satellite helped measure the age of the universe.

LOCAL LONG DISTANCE

The universe is so vast, we must measure it by compairing it to a distance we can understand. One Astronomical Unit (AU) is equal to the average distance between the Sun and Earth—93 million miles (149.6 million km).

The farthest human-made object from Earth is the Voyager I space probe, which is 130 AU away at the edge of our **solar system**.

THINKING BIGGER...

To measure larger distances, scientists use **light-years**. This is the distance that light travels in a year—almost 5,878,499,810,000 miles (9,460,528,404,847 km). Besides the Sun, the nearest star to earth is Proxima Centauri, which is approximately 271,000 AU or 4.24 light-years away.

...AND BIGGER

It takes just 1.3 seconds for light to travel between the Moon and Earth. In contrast, it takes light 100,000 years to cross our home galaxy, the Milky Way. The Milky Way is just one of billions of galaxies, separated by millions of light-years of space.

WHAT'S SPACE LIKE?

We imagine space as being empty, but it actually contains very thinly spread **molecules** of gas and dust. Space close to a star may be warmed up by the star's heat energy but it is seriously cold everywhere else, with an average temperature of -454.36 °F (-270.2 °C).

Shhhh!

In space no one can hear you scream... or make any sound, for that matter. Sound travels in waves by making molecules of **matter** vibrate. In the large empty areas of space, there are very few molecules to vibrate, so there is just silence.

93 BILLION

= THE NUMBER OF LIGHT-YEARS IT WOULD TAKE TO CROSS THE OBSERVABLE UNIVERSE ACCORDING TO THE EUROPEAN SPACE AGENCY (ESA)

INVESTIGATING THE UNIVERSE

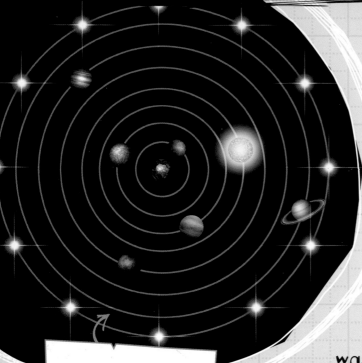

Ptolemy's model of the universe

In the past, religion tried to explain the great mysteries of space. Over time, scientific advances have helped us learn a great deal about the universe and how it works.

Self-Centered

For over 1,500 years, many people agreed with the Egyptian scientist Ptolemy, who thought that Earth was the center of the universe. This view was challenged by Islamic scholars in the Middle Ages, and by the Polish astronomer Nicolaus Copernicus in 1543. Copernicus proposed that Earth and other planets traveled around the Sun, but he still placed our solar system at the center of the universe.

Burning Issue

The Italian philosopher, Giordano Bruno was one of the first to state that the solar system was just one of many star systems in space. He also believed that people lived on other planets! His views brought him into conflict with the Church and in 1600, he was burned at the stake for his beliefs.

THINKING AHEAD

Many advances in astronomy were made before telescopes. In 1687, English physicist Isaac Newton presented his theory of how **gravity** affects every object in the universe. German philosopher Immanuel Kant suggested 70 years later that the solar system formed from disks of spinning dust and gas.

Fuzzy Thinking

After telescopes were invented in the 1600s, astronomers discovered new objects in space—fuzzy spiral shapes containing pinpoints of bright light. These were originally called nebulae, meaning clouds, but science would later show that they were star-packed galaxies.

GALACTIC BREAKTHROUGH

Until the 1900s, most scientists thought the Milky Way contained the entire universe. This all changed when American astronomer Edwin Hubble measured objects using a giant 8.2 foot (2.5 m) telescope. He found that the objects were 10 times farther away than the most distant stars in the Milky Way. He was looking into another galaxy–Andromeda–thus proving that other galaxies exist.

Modern advances in technology have helped us to investigate space. The Illustris **simulation**, shown here, used 8,000 powerful computer chips to produce a model of how galaxies may have formed.

2,000
= THE NUMBER OF YEARS IT WOULD TAKE A HOME COMPUTER TO MAKE AS MANY CALCULATIONS AS THE ILLUSTRIS SIMULATION OF THE UNIVERSE

HOW THE UNIVERSE BEGAN

The Big Bang **theory is the most commonly accepted idea of how the universe began. It states that the universe and everything it now contains emerged from a single point. Energy, matter, and time simply did not exist before the Big Bang.**

Coming Up With The Big Bang

Discoveries in the early 1900s showed that galaxies were moving away from each other. This means that the universe is expanding. Georges Lemaître suggested that if the universe is increasing in size, then it must have been smaller in the past. This led him to conclude that the universe began out of a single point. His ideas, published in 1927-1931, formed the basis of the Big Bang theory.

Georges Lemaître (1894-1966) was a Belgian priest and scientist.

This photo shows the cosmic background radiation present 375,000 years after the Big Bang. Hot spots are red and the cold spots are dark blue.

IN THE BACKGROUND

The Big Bang theory states that after the Big Bang, energy traveled through the young universe before cooling and fading into the background. This idea is supported by scientific evidence, since **cosmic background radiation** is the oldest energy that scientists are able to observe.

Pigeon Poop

In 1964 two young scientists, Robert Wilson and Arno Penzias, were the first to discover cosmic background radiation. While cleaning out a radio antenna dish that was full of pigeons and pigeon droppings, they detected low-level radio noise. This proved to be background radiation from the Big Bang.

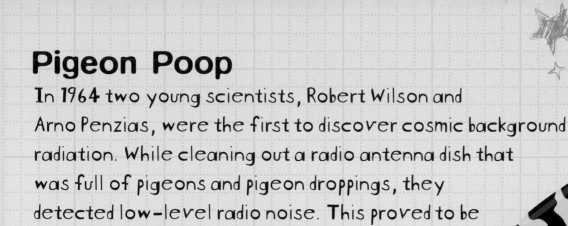

RECREATING THE MOMENT

We cannot look back at the very moment of the Big Bang, so theories come from mathematical models and experiments like the Large Hadron Collider (LHC). The LHC is a machine that sends particles of atoms whizzing down a 10 mile (27 km) long tunnel at almost the **speed of light**. The atoms smash into each other to simulate the conditions that took place shortly after the Big Bang.

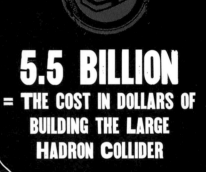

5.5 BILLION
= THE COST IN DOLLARS OF BUILDING THE LARGE HADRON COLLIDER

The Large Hadron Collider

DEVELOPMENT AND FORMATION

Strap yourself in. You're about to go on the wildest ride imaginable, starting at the very beginning of the universe.

Not Exactly A Bang

The universe didn't explode, but rather expanded—at a truly incredible rate. Scientists estimate that in a tiny fraction of a second, it went from something smaller than an atom to something bigger than an entire galaxy. It continued to grow to trillions and trillions of its original size.

WHEN DID THE FIRST GALAXIES FORM?

No one is certain. It was once thought that galaxies didn't form for the first billion years. However, in 2011, the Hubble Space Telescope discovered the oldest known galaxy, estimated to have formed around 500 million years after the Big Bang.

The Formation Of The Universe

In the briefest of moments, the universe expanded at an amazing rate. Just after the Big Bang, the universe was so hot that any particles that managed to form were instantly destroyed.

380,000 years

After around 380,000 years, the universe had cooled down to about 5,432 °F (3,000 °C). Hydrogen and helium atoms managed to form. The universe continued to expand but not as rapidly as before.

400 million years

From around 400,000 years to about 400 million years after the Big Bang, the universe was a dark, foggy place.

Around 400 million years after the Big Bang, the first stars, called protostars, began to develop. Eventually, these protostars began to carry out **nuclear fusion** in their cores and started shining brightly.

9 billion years

Our solar system was created around 4.6 billion years ago, more than 9 billion years after the Big Bang. First, the Sun formed from a large cloud of gas and dust. As it developed, a large disk of leftover gas and dust grew around it, eventually creating the planets and other parts of the solar system.

13.7 billion years (present day)

THE EXPANDING UNIVERSE

In 1929, Edwin Hubble discovered something fundamental with his space telescope about the universe: it was still expanding! This breakthrough reinforced the Big Bang theory and has been studied by scientists ever since.

Redshift

Remember the last time a police car drove past you with its siren blaring? The sound is high pitched as it travels toward you and lower pitched as it drives away. This is called the Doppler effect. A similar thing known as redshift happens with light.

EDWIN'S WIN-WIN

Hubble figured out that galaxies were moving away from the solar system by measuring distances and using redshift. He found that the farther a galaxy lay from Earth, the faster it was moving away. His conclusion was that the entire universe was expanding.

A redshift
When an object moves away, its light waves are stretched out and the object appears red.

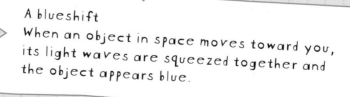

A blueshift
When an object in space moves toward you, its light waves are squeezed together and the object appears blue.

The Hubble Constant

Hubble estimated the speed at which the universe was expanding, which is known as the Hubble constant. Today, the Hubble constant is thought to be around 44 miles per second (71 kms) for every 3.26 million light-years (mly) a galaxy lies away from us.

WHAT'S THE UNIVERSE EXPANDING INTO?

It isn't expanding into anything. Space within the universe is expanding, getting bigger between the galaxies. It is a bit like making chocolate chip cookies. The chips (galaxies) start close to each other but as the cookies are baked and expand, the chips move away from each other.

FARTHER AND FASTER

Because the universe is expanding, the farther away a galaxy is, the faster it is moving. A galaxy 3.26 mly away from us is moving away at a speed of 44 mps (71 kms). However, a galaxy 100 times farther away (326 mly) is moving 100 times faster, giving it a speed of 4,412 mps (7,100 kms). Whoosh!

The way that cookies expand when they are baking gives you an idea of the way the universe is expanding.

GROUPS, CLUSTERS, AND SUPERCLUSTERS

Gravity often pulls several galaxies together into groups. Large groups made up of many galaxies are called clusters. The number of galaxies in a cluster can range from a few to several thousand.

The Local Group

The Milky Way is part of the Local Group, a collection of over 30 galaxies. Andromeda is the biggest galaxy in the Local Group, containing more than twice the number of stars found in the Milky Way. At the other end of the scale is the Ursa Minor Dwarf, which is less than ten light-years across but contains many ancient stars.

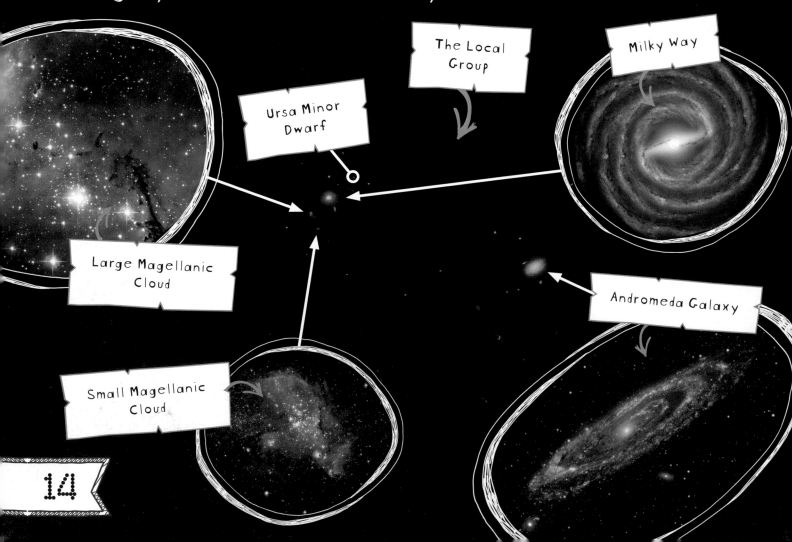

The Local Group

Milky Way

Ursa Minor Dwarf

Large Magellanic Cloud

Small Magellanic Cloud

Andromeda Galaxy

Neighboring Clusters

The largest nearby cluster of galaxies is the Virgo Cluster. This cluster covers an area of approximately 10 million light-years. It contains around 160 large galaxies, including the giant elliptical galaxy M87.

COLLIDING CLUSTER

One of the smallest clusters contains just five galaxies. Stephan's Quintet is about 280 million light-years away from us. Four of its five galaxies are locked in a gigantic collision, creating a shock wave bigger in size than the Milky Way!

Two of the galaxies in Stephan's Quintet are so close that they look like one galaxy.

WHAT IS A SUPERCLUSTER?

A supercluster is a cluster of clusters. These can contain hundreds of galaxy clusters and are unimaginably large. The Local Group, Virgo Cluster, and around another 100 groups and clusters are all part of the Laniakea Supercluster.

160 MILLION
= THE DIAMETER IN LIGHT–YEARS OF THE LANIAKEA SUPERCLUSTER.

BLACK HOLES

Black holes **are one of the most fascinating and terrifying features of the universe. They are mysterious, invisible objects that gobble up stars, planets, and even galaxies.**

Super Dense

A black hole is anything but an empty hole. It is an area that packs a huge amount of material, or **mass**, into a very small space, creating an unbelievably **dense** object. The more mass an object has, the more gravity it exerts on other objects. A black hole has an enormous amount of gravity, pulling everything into it.

STELLAR BLACK HOLES

Stellar black holes start out as large stars, which are ripped apart by a giant explosion called a supernova. After the explosion, the core of the star collapses in on itself. If the core has enough mass, then gravity will keep on pulling in on itself until a black hole is formed.

Stellar black hole

Accretion disk—Matter often forms a spinning disk around a black hole as it is pulled toward it.

Event horizon—This is the point of no return for matter pulled toward a black hole.

Singularity—The entire mass of a black hole is contained within a single point in space.

On The Horizon

You don't want to be anywhere near a black hole's event horizon. This is the boundary line that marks a region of space around a black hole. Nothing can escape from this boundary. Everything within the event horizon, from the smallest dust particles to entire stars, will be pulled into the black hole and crushed by its extreme gravity.

24,000
= THE NUMBER OF LIGHT-YEARS FROM EARTH THAT THE NEAREST KNOWN BLACK HOLE, SAGITTARIUS A*, LIES.

The black hole at the center of the NGC 1097 galaxy has a mass 100 million times larger than the Sun's.

Black hole

SUPERMASSIVE BLACK HOLES
Supermassive black holes have far greater mass than stellar black holes. Scientists are unsure how they form, but they believe that most galaxies have a supermassive black hole at their center. The black hole at the center of the Milky Way galaxy is called Sagittarius A*. It has a mass equal to about 4.3 million Suns.

BLACK-HOLE HUNTERS

Astronomers search for black holes in many ways. They look for gaps where something should be in space. They study the behavior of stars and other bodies. They can also detect X-rays, a kind of energy that travels through space, which are given off by matter near black holes.

Tell-Tale Signs

Black-hole hunters keep their eyes peeled for visible objects in space behaving as if a giant object were nearby. This could be a star wobbling as it travels through space or a disk of matter spinning around an invisible center.

Launched in 2012, NuSTAR is the first telescope in space that can focus X-rays into sharp images.

HDE 226868

BLACK HOLE: CONFIRMED!

The first black hole to be discovered and confirmed was Cygnus X-1, about 10,000 light-years from Earth. X-rays given off by Cygnus X-1 were spotted in 1971 by NASA's Uhuru telescope, the first telescope dedicated to detecting X-rays in space.

Cygnus X-1 is dragging in material from the nearby star HDE 226868 due to the strong pull of its gravity.

Double Trouble

A small number of galaxies, including NGC 6240, have not one but two supermassive black holes at their center. Astronomers believe that this happens when two galaxies merge into one. Despite their huge mass, the black holes orbit each other at speeds of up to 5 million mph (8 million km/h).

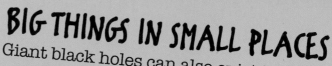

BIG THINGS IN SMALL PLACES

Giant black holes can also exist in small galaxies. M60-UCD1 is a dwarf galaxy with a tiny diameter of just 300 light-years. Yet, in 2014, the Hubble Space Telescope discovered a monstrous black hole at its center, with the mass of 20 million Suns!

Give Us A Tune

A black hole found in the Perseus galaxy cluster has been sounding out the lowest note in the universe —a B flat, 57 octaves below middle C.

HOW BIG IS THE BIGGEST SUPERMASSIVE BLACK HOLE?

The largest one found so far is a truly gigantic supermassive black hole at the center of the NGC 4889 galaxy. It has a mass equal to about 21 billion Suns!

supermassive black holes

Eventually, NGC 6240's two supermassive black holes will probably merge into one.

ACTIVE GALAXIES

The light that astronomers observe from regular galaxies, such as Andromeda, comes from stars within the galaxy. Active galaxies are different. They generate energy in tiny areas near their centers, known as the galactic nuclei.

Not Jet Set

Scientists think that all active galaxies are powered by black holes at their center. Some active galaxies, known as radio galaxies, don't just pull in matter. They also spit out large jets of material at superfast speeds. This material cools down in space, forming enormous plumes of gas.

GIANT PLUMES

Centaurus A is a huge, elliptical radio galaxy, formed when two galaxies merged millions of years ago. It's around 12 million light-years away, but it is the fifth-brightest galaxy in the night sky viewed from Earth. Its two giant jets are over a million light-years long.

Centaurus A

Gas Plume

Quasars

Quasars are extremely bright objects found in distant galaxies. Many are located 9–12 billion light-years away. Yes, quasars can be studied on Earth because they send out vast amounts of energy, much of it as visible light.

Quasars are like flashlights that shine as bright as a whole city. Their light drowns out the light from the other stars in their galaxy.

4 TRILLION

= THE NUMBER OF TIMES MORE BRIGHT THE 3C 273 QUASAR SHINES THAN THE SUN. DISCOVERED IN THE 1960S, IT WAS THE FIRST QUASAR EVER IDENTIFIED.

IT'S HUGE!

A stunning cluster of 73 quasars has been discovered about 9 billion light-years from us. Called the Huge Large Quasar Group, it is so big that it would take a spacecraft traveling at the speed of light 4 billion years to cross it. Some scientists believe it is the largest structure in the universe.

DARK MATTER AND DARK ENERGY

Astronomers have learned much about the universe, but many questions remain unanswered. Two of the biggest questions concern things we have not yet been able to observe—the deeply mysterious dark matter and dark energy.

A Dark-Matter Mystery

Scientists don't think there's enough regular matter to explain the amount of gravity present in the universe. This suggests that the universe must contain a different type of matter, one that doesn't absorb or give out light or other waves, making it invisible. This is known as dark matter. Scientists think it might make up more than 80% of all the matter in the universe.

WHAT IS MATTER?

Matter is formed of atoms, occupies space, and has mass. Matter makes up everything in the universe, from a tube of toothpaste to a giant star. All objects made of matter exert gravity on other objects.

This is an artist's idea of what dark matter might look like, if we could see it.

WIMP!

What could dark matter be? One theory is called Weakly Interacting Massive Particles (WIMPs). It states that particles, which are tiny bits of matter, would pass through ordinary matter without effecting it. If WIMPs were present everywhere in the universe, they might all add up to the missing amount of matter. However, experiments to find WIMPs have been unsuccessful so far.

One WIMP experiment placed a detector filled with low-pressure gas 3,600 feet (1,100 m) underground in a mine. The higher layers of rock absorbed other rays from the universe. Scientists thought that WIMPs might pass through the rock into the detector, where they might collide with the gas particles. Unfortunately, no WIMPs were detected.

DARK ENERGY

In the 1990s, scientists discovered that the universe is expanding at a quicker rate than in the past. They concluded that some other force must be overcoming the force of gravity, which draws objects toward each other. An unknown energy must be powering this increase in expansion speed. Scientists call this mysterious force dark energy.

Other rays from the universe

Rock

Possible path of WIMPs

Rays absorbed by the rock

Mine shaft

Gas filled WIMP detector

23

ODDITIES OF THE UNIVERSE

Dark matter and dark energy are not the only weird things found in the universe. Check out this collection of seriously strange bodies and phenomena **that surprise and mystify scientists.**

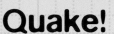
starquake

Quake!

Magnetars are a type of large star responsible for earthquake-like tremors in space, known as starquakes. In 2004, a starquake from SGR 1806-20 was so powerful that some of its effects reached Earth's atmosphere from over a distance of 50,000 light-years away.

SGR 1806-20's starquake lasted less than a second, yet released more energy than the Sun releases in 100,000 years!

A TRUE SHOOTING STAR

What we call shooting stars are meteoroids—small pieces of rock or metal that burn up in Earth's atmosphere. One real star, however, is shooting through space at the incredibly high speed of 291,000 miles per hour (468,000 km/h). Mira is about the same size as the Sun, but it is getting smaller because it loses gas as it whizzes through space.

Mira is the only known star with a long tail.

= THE LENGTH OF MIRA'S TAIL IN LIGHT-YEARS
13

Green Gas

In 2007, a Dutch schoolteacher, Hanny van Arkel, discovered a strange, glowing, blue-green blob of gas floating in space close to a spiral galaxy. Named Hanny's Voorwerp (meaning Hanny's object), this is no small cloud. It's roughly the size of the Milky Way!

spiral galaxy

Hanny's Voorwerp

Fruit Loopy
Scientists have discovered a dust and gas cloud around 26,000 light-years away. Named Sagittarius B2, this cloud is full of ethyl formate, the chemical that gives raspberries their fruity flavor.

WATER, WATER
The universe's biggest known reservoir of water isn't on Earth. It surrounds a quasar over 12 billion light-years away. The APM 08279+5255 quasar is surrounded by a giant disk of water vapor that contains 140 billion times more water than Earth's oceans!

IS THERE ANYONE OUT THERE?

The universe is unimaginably vast. Can Earth really be the only place where intelligent life exists? While no signs of extraterrestrial (meaning beyond Earth) life have been found so far, some scientists remain hopeful that contact will be made one day.

A Message From Earth

Other star systems are too far away for human spaceflight to reach, so scientists have tried other ways of making contact. For example, Pioneer 10 and 11 are space probes, or robotic spacecraft, launched into space carrying pictures of humans, as well as a map of our solar system and its location in the Milky Way.

The Voyager gold record is engraved with information about how to play the disk.

GOING FOR GOLD

The Voyager 1 and 2 space probes carried gold records containing sounds from Earth, as well as spoken greetings in 55 different languages. The probes are now the farthest machines from Earth; Voyager 1 has actually left our solar system and is now over 12 billion miles (19 billion km) away.

2 MILLION
= THE NUMBER OF YEARS IT WILL TAKE PIONEER 10 TO GET CLOSE TO THE NEXT STAR IN ITS PATH, THE STAR ALDEBARAN

New Worlds

Advances in astronomy have led to the discovery of over 1,800 planets orbiting stars other than our Sun. Called exoplanets, some may orbit their star at the right distance for water in a liquid form to be present—a necessity for life to flourish.

Kepler-186f is the first Earth-sized planet to be found orbiting a star at a distance at which liquid water might be present on the planet's surface.

LISTENING IN

Instead of sending out signals, some alien-hunting projects scan the skies for possible signals from intelligent life outside the solar system. The Allen Telescope Array is a series of 42 radio telescopes that work together to seek out radio signals from deep space.

WHAT WAS THE ARECIBO MESSAGE?

In 1974, a message was beamed out in radio waves from the Arecibo radio telescope dish in Puerto Rico toward a cluster of stars about 21,000 light-years away. The radio message shows simple block pictures of the Arecibo dish, our solar system, and the key chemicals that make life possible on Earth.

Hi!

In 1967, researcher Jocelyn Bell discovered regular radio signals from space. She named the signals LGM-1, short for Little Green Men. It turned out the signals were actually coming from the first pulsar star ever discovered.

HOW WILL IT ALL END?

First of all, relax. The universe probably has trillions of years to go before it ends, if it ever does. Cosmologists puzzle over what the distant future holds for the universe and have developed a number of theories.

Chilled Out

The Big Chill theory suggests that if the universe continued to expand forever, the void, or empty space, between galaxies would grow until they became lonely islands in space. The galaxies would run out of gas to make new stars, and existing stars would eventually use up their energy and die. The universe would end up as a cold, dark wasteland.

WHAT SHAPE IS THE UNIVERSE?

No one knows. Various shapes have been proposed from a curved, saddle-like shape to a sphere and even a ring donut! Cosmologists wonder whether the universe is infinite, meaning it continues forever, or whether it is finite and has a definite shape.

THE BIG RIP

In 2003, a new idea for how the universe might end was published. It suggested that the universe will keep on getting bigger, but at a faster and faster rate. As the universe expands more and more rapidly, it will overcome the gravity that holds everything together, ripping all matter apart.

The universe's shape, and whether it is finite or infinite, might determine how it ends, if at all.

The Big Crunch

An alternative ending for the universe sees it stop expanding at a moment in the very distant future. At that point, the force of gravity overcomes the force of expansion and begins pulling everything together. Galaxies would speed toward each other, colliding and merging as the universe shrinks. Eventually, it would collapse and fall inward on itself to a single point.

The present universe

Time

The big crunch

BOUNCING BACK

The Big Crunch might not be the end of the story, though. From that single point, it might be possible for a new Big Bang to cause another, quite different universe to emerge. This idea is known as the Big Bounce.

The Big Crunch might be like the Big Bang but in reverse. Scientists currently think there needs to be a lot more matter in the universe for the Big Crunch to be the likely ending.

The Big Bounce theory

The universe gets to a single point.

The universe starts to collapse.

A new universe starts to expand.

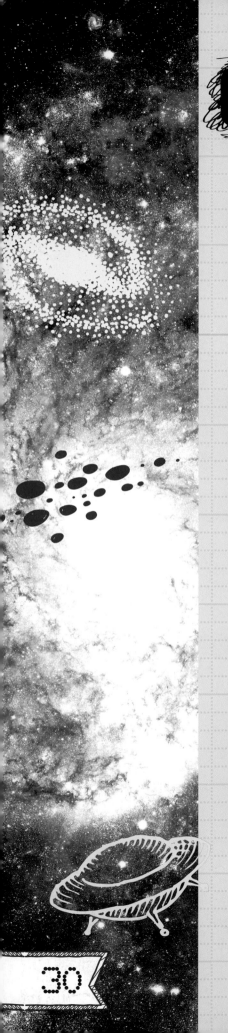

GLOSSARY

atom The smallest unit of matter

Big Bang The theory of how the universe formed out of a single point around 13.7 billion years ago

black hole An object in space with such strong gravity that nothing nearby can escape its pull, including light

cosmic background radiation Radiation, possibly originating shortly after the Big Bang, that is moving in every direction

cosmologist Someone that studies the beginning, structure, and space/time relationship of the universe

dense Containing a lot of matter inside a small space

galaxy An enormous collection of stars, planets, and clouds of dust and gases, all kept together by gravity

gravity The invisible force of attraction between objects

light-year The distance traveled by light in a year—6 trillion miles (9.6 trillion kilometers)

mass How much matter an object contains

matter Physical things that take up space and have mass, such as solids, liquids, or gases

molecule The smallest unit of a substance that is composed of two or more atoms

nuclear fusion The process inside a star that joins the centers of hydrogen atoms together to form helium, generating energy

phenomena A fact or occurrence that can be observed

simulation A representation of a system used to examine a problem

solar system A star being orbited by planets, moons, asteroids, or comets

speed of light The speed at which light travels through space—186,282 miles per second (299,792 km/s)

FURTHER INFORMATION

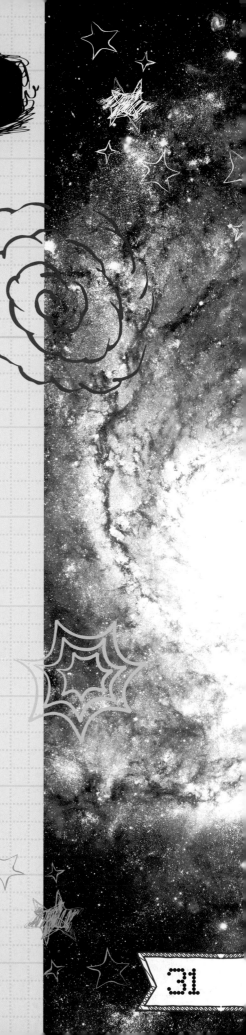

Books

Beyond the Solar System: Exploring Galaxies, Black Holes, Alien Planets, and More; A History with 21 Activities
by Mary Kay Carson (Chicago Review Press, 2013)

The Story of Space: Looking Beyond
by Steve Parker (Franklin Watts, 2015)

Exploring Black Holes
by Laura Waxman (Lerner, 2012)

Websites

www.nasa.gov/audience/forstudents/9-12/features/
 what-is-dark-matter.html
NASA explains dark matter and how it is studied.

http://science.nationalgeographic.com/science/
 space/universe/
This National Geographic site provides a deeper look into outer space with amazing images and information about the universe.

http://hubblesite.org/hubble_discoveries/dark_energy
A web presentation from the Hubble Space Telescope team explains how scientists first encountered the mystery of dark energy.

INDEX